I0007817

Cursor AI

Expert Tips for Developers and Beginners

Unlock 159% Faster Development and

Boost Efficiency with Artificial

Intelligence Powered Coding Tools

Jason M. Scott

Table of contents

Introduction

In recent years, artificial intelligence has permeated nearly every aspect of modern life, from automating daily tasks to enhancing decision-making in industries. However, its impact on the world of coding and software development is especially transformative. Developers are constantly seeking ways to streamline workflows, reduce errors, and boost productivity, and AI has proven to be a game-changer in this arena. Imagine writing code at lightning speed, fixing bugs with minimal effort, and building entire features without spending hours combing through documentation or internet forums. This is no longer a distant future—it's a reality, thanks to AI tools like Cursor AI.

Cursor AI represents a new era in software development. While it functions similarly to popular code editors like Visual Studio Code, its power lies in the built-in AI features that elevate it beyond a traditional editor. Cursor AI doesn't just help you write code; it assists you in optimizing, iterating, and even debugging in real time. The integration of AI into the coding process means developers can now work faster and more efficiently, allowing them to focus on creativity and problem-solving rather than repetitive tasks. Cursor AI has proven to make coding up to 2.5 times faster for experienced developers, a significant boost in productivity that can make or break project timelines.

This book serves as a guide to unlocking the full potential of Cursor AI. Whether you're a seasoned developer or someone just starting out, this book is designed to help you understand how to make the most of this revolutionary tool. You'll learn not only how to use Cursor AI but also how to integrate it into your daily workflow in a way that transforms your approach to coding. From understanding its core features to maximizing its advanced functionalities, this guide will provide you with everything you need to know to code faster, smarter, and more efficiently.

Chapter 1: Setting Up Cursor AI

Downloading and Installing Cursor AI: Getting started with Cursor AI is remarkably simple, but the real value lies in understanding the benefits of its features from the outset. To begin, you'll need to visit Cursor AI's official website at cursor.com, where you can easily find the download link for the software. Cursor AI is built on the familiar Visual Studio Code platform, so if you've used VS Code before, the installation process will feel straightforward. For those who haven't, the installation steps are still intuitive.

Once you're on the website, click the "Download" button. The software is compatible with most major operating systems, including Windows, macOS, and Linux. After the download is complete, follow the on-screen instructions to install the application on your machine. The installation process should take only a few minutes, depending on your system.

Now, while the free version of Cursor AI offers a solid introduction to the tool's capabilities, unlocking its full potential requires an upgrade to the pro plan, priced at $20 per month. This plan grants you access to more advanced features and more robust AI models, such as OpenAI's GPT-4 and Anthropic's Claude 3.5. If you're a frequent user of AI tools like ChatGPT, you'll notice a significant improvement in speed and functionality, making the pro plan a worthwhile investment. The additional features and nearly unlimited usage will not only pay for themselves over time but will also provide a seamless coding experience, allowing you to fully harness Cursor AI's capabilities.

Once installed, you'll be ready to dive into the world of AI-powered coding, and from there, the setup process is much like Visual Studio Code. You can choose your preferred theme, import any plugins you're already using, and integrate API keys from external services, such as OpenAI or Anthropic, for added flexibility. With Cursor AI installed and configured, you're ready to explore a whole new approach to writing and managing code efficiently.

The VS Code Familiarity Factor: One of the standout features of Cursor AI is its close resemblance to Visual Studio Code, a popular code editor used by millions of developers worldwide. This similarity makes transitioning to Cursor AI incredibly smooth, especially for those already familiar with VS Code. If you've spent time working in Visual Studio Code, you'll feel right at home in Cursor AI. From the layout to the key commands, much of the interface mirrors what VS Code users have come to expect, reducing the learning curve considerably.

The familiar features are all there—the sidebar for file navigation, the terminal integration, and the ability to install extensions. Cursor AI even supports many of the plugins you might already be using with VS Code, making the switch seamless. You won't have to sacrifice the customizations and setups you've built in Visual Studio Code because most can be imported directly into Cursor AI, allowing you to maintain a consistent work environment.

The key difference, however, is the addition of Cursor AI's powerful built-in AI features. While the structure may feel the same as VS Code, Cursor AI introduces tools like real-time AI-assisted coding and advanced troubleshooting, which enhance the development process in ways Visual Studio Code cannot match on its own. With this added layer of intelligence, Cursor AI takes what VS Code offers and elevates it to a more efficient, smarter platform. For developers who want to maintain their comfort with Visual Studio Code's structure but crave the enhanced productivity AI offers, Cursor AI becomes a natural and powerful extension of what they already know.

Configuring your Workspace: Once Cursor AI is installed, setting up your workspace is the next step to ensure you have a personalized and smooth coding experience. Much like Visual Studio Code, Cursor AI offers a range of customization options, allowing you to configure your environment to match your workflow preferences. This process involves selecting themes, installing plugins, and integrating APIs, all of which can enhance your productivity and streamline your development process.

To start, choose a theme that suits your visual preferences. Cursor AI comes with a variety of default themes, both light and dark, but if you're used to a specific theme from Visual Studio Code, you can easily import it into Cursor AI. Whether you prefer a minimalist layout or a high-contrast design, setting the right theme can make your workspace feel familiar and reduce eye strain during long coding sessions.

Next, consider the plugins you need. Since Cursor AI is built on the same foundation as Visual Studio Code, most of the plugins you've relied on can be carried over. From language-specific support to version control extensions like Git, the ecosystem is vast. You can access the plugin marketplace directly within Cursor AI and install the tools you need to boost your workflow. Popular plugins like Prettier for code formatting or ESLint for JavaScript linting can be quickly added to ensure your code stays clean and adheres to best practices.

A key strength of Cursor AI lies in its ability to integrate with external APIs, enhancing the AI-powered features that come with the pro plan. If you're using external AI services, such as OpenAI's GPT models or Anthropic's Claude, you can easily bring in their API keys for use directly within Cursor AI. By integrating these APIs, Cursor AI will be able to pull data and provide even more powerful suggestions as you code. This not only makes Cursor AI a highly adaptable tool but also allows you to leverage cutting-edge AI models beyond what's built into the software.

With your workspace configured—complete with personalized themes, powerful plugins, and AI integrations—you're set to experience coding in a more efficient, intuitive, and intelligent way. Each of these elements plays a role in tailoring the environment to meet your specific needs, ensuring that your experience with Cursor AI is smooth and productive from day one.

Chapter 2: Understanding Cursor AI's Key Features

AI-Enhanced Coding: Cursor AI is designed to fundamentally change how developers approach coding by integrating AI tools directly into the workflow. This goes beyond the typical code editor features, offering an intelligent assistant that can anticipate needs, suggest improvements, and automate time-consuming tasks. The real beauty of Cursor AI lies in how it enhances coding speed, allowing developers to work faster without sacrificing quality. Whether you're writing new code, debugging, or iterating on existing features, Cursor AI can shave off hours of work through its AI-powered capabilities.

At the core of Cursor AI's speed advantage is its ability to assist in real-time. Rather than manually searching for solutions, navigating through documentation, or scouring online forums for examples, developers can use the AI features to generate suggestions instantly. For example, while coding, you can highlight a section of your code and press a hotkey, such as Control K, to bring up AI suggestions. Cursor analyzes the context of your code and offers edits, improvements, or alternative approaches, dramatically reducing the time spent refining and optimizing.

The AI tools are also capable of making bulk edits that might normally take significant time and effort. Rather than going line by line to tweak parameters or adjust formatting, Cursor AI allows you to issue a single command and have the AI apply changes across your project. This level of automation doesn't just save time—it eliminates repetitive tasks that can bog down even the most experienced developer. In this way, the coding process becomes more about supervising the AI's work and less about writing each piece from scratch.

Another significant speed benefit comes from Cursor's ability to learn from your entire codebase. When you open a project in Cursor AI, it indexes all of the files so that it can reference them when making suggestions. This means that the AI doesn't just operate in isolation on a single file; it understands how each part of your project interacts, allowing it to make intelligent decisions when applying changes. This awareness prevents errors and speeds up the debugging process, as the AI can suggest fixes that take the entire project's structure into account.

For experienced developers, Cursor AI can make coding up to 2.5 times faster. In real-world applications, this has translated into significant time savings, particularly when building new features or iterating on complex projects. By automating routine tasks, enhancing code quality through intelligent suggestions, and speeding up the process of debugging, Cursor AI allows developers to focus on higher-level problem solving and creativity. This shift in how coding is approached is at the heart of Cursor AI's transformative power in the development space.

Control K & Control L Functions: Cursor AI's standout functionality is its ability to enhance coding through the intelligent use of hotkeys, particularly the Control K and Control L commands. These features allow developers to seamlessly interact with the AI, transforming how they write, modify, and improve their code in real-time. By making coding feel more like a dialogue between you and the AI, Cursor empowers you to work smarter and faster, cutting out many of the time-consuming steps traditionally required in the development process.

The Control K function is designed for precise, focused edits. Imagine you're working on a feature and realize that you want to make a small change—like adjusting the padding of a button or modifying the color scheme of a component. Rather than manually combing through the code to make these changes, you can simply highlight the relevant section and press Control K. This command brings up a prompt where you can instruct the AI on what you'd like to change. For example, if you want to add more padding to a button, you might write "add more padding to this button." The AI then analyzes the highlighted code and makes the necessary adjustments based on your instructions. It acts like an extra set of eyes and hands, quickly applying changes while keeping the code's structure intact.

What's particularly powerful about Control K is its ability to make these changes in a way that feels natural. You can think of it as reviewing pull requests from an AI teammate. Once the AI suggests an edit, you have the option to accept or reject it, giving you control over the final output. And if you're not satisfied with the changes, you can undo them with a simple press of Control Z. This means that the AI enhances your coding without ever taking full control, allowing you to maintain oversight and make sure the changes align with your intentions.

While Control K is great for small, targeted adjustments, the Control L function takes things to a whole new level. Pressing Control L opens a chat window where you can interact with the AI in a more conversational way, similar to using ChatGPT but integrated directly into your coding environment. What sets this feature apart is that Cursor AI already knows the context of your project because it has indexed all the files in your codebase. So when you ask for suggestions or changes, the AI can make decisions based on the entire scope of your project, rather than just the file you're working on.

For example, if you want to reorganize a user interface, you can describe what you want—perhaps moving a QR code to the left of the screen and shifting text to the right. The AI processes this request and makes the appropriate changes across the relevant files. It also allows you to refine your requests within the same chat, so you can iterate quickly. If the AI's first attempt isn't quite right, you can give it feedback, like "this looks great, but can you make the menu disappear when I click away?" The AI responds in real time, making further adjustments until you're satisfied with the result.

These two functions, Control K for specific tweaks and Control L for more comprehensive changes, make coding with Cursor AI feel like a collaborative process. Rather than manually coding every detail, you can focus on the bigger picture, letting the AI handle the repetitive or complex changes while you steer the overall direction of the project. This intelligent collaboration is what truly sets Cursor AI apart from traditional code editors, making it an invaluable tool for developers looking to maximize efficiency and streamline their workflows.

The Chat Window and Codebase Indexing: The chat window in Cursor AI is one of its most powerful tools, designed to facilitate a dynamic and interactive coding process. When you open a project, Cursor doesn't just see the individual file you're working on—it indexes the entire codebase, giving it a complete understanding of how all your files interact. This allows the AI to provide suggestions and make changes that take into account the full scope of your project, not just isolated pieces of code.

The chat window is essentially your gateway to this advanced AI functionality. When you press Control L, the window appears on the right side of your screen, allowing you to type in prompts, ask for changes, or troubleshoot issues in a conversational manner. It functions much like ChatGPT but is tailored to the context of your code, meaning it has a deeper understanding of what you're working on. For instance, you can ask it to refactor a specific function, add a new feature, or even debug a problem across multiple files, and it will generate suggestions that are directly relevant to your entire project.

One of the standout features of the chat window is its ability to reference specific files. When you open a project, Cursor indexes all the files, meaning that the AI can look across the entire codebase to make informed decisions. For example, if you're working on a front-end file that interacts with a back-end API, the AI will understand the connection between those files and provide suggestions that maintain the integrity of both sides. This is particularly useful when making significant changes, as the AI ensures that nothing gets overlooked or broken in the process.

However, with such a powerful tool, there can be instances where too much context might lead to confusion, especially when working on large projects with hundreds of files. To avoid this, Cursor AI gives you control over which files it references. You can specify which parts of the codebase the AI should focus on, reducing the risk of it pulling in unnecessary or irrelevant files. This can be particularly helpful when you want to make changes to just a few files or a specific feature without the AI considering the entire project.

For instance, if you're adding a new feature to a single component of your project, you can limit the AI's focus to that component and its related files. By narrowing the scope of its search, you prevent the AI from getting bogged down by unrelated sections of the codebase, ensuring that it only draws from the most relevant sources.

This also helps you maintain control over the AI's outputs, as you can guide it toward the right parts of your project.

In practice, this functionality streamlines complex coding tasks, such as refactoring or adding new features, where multiple files need to be updated simultaneously. Instead of having to manually track down every file that needs adjusting, Cursor AI can handle that for you, referencing the codebase and making sure everything aligns. It also allows you to toggle between broad and narrow contexts, giving you the flexibility to either let the AI draw from the whole project or zero in on specific files.

The chat window's intuitive design, combined with Cursor AI's powerful codebase indexing, creates a seamless way to interact with your project. Whether you're making quick edits or undertaking large-scale refactoring, the chat window helps you navigate the complexity of coding with ease, while ensuring that the AI operates within the boundaries you set. This makes coding with Cursor not only faster but also smarter, as you leverage the full power of AI while staying in control of your project's integrity.

Chapter 3: Real-World Application: Building "QR Contact"

Building a Simple App Twice: To truly understand how transformative Cursor AI can be, let's explore an example that highlights its impact on both speed and efficiency. Imagine building a simple app twice—once using traditional coding methods and once using Cursor AI. For this comparison, we'll use a simple project: creating an app that generates and shares contact information via QR codes. This will allow us to see the difference Cursor AI makes when it comes to development time, ease of use, and overall productivity.

In the first version of the app, we'll follow the conventional method. Writing the app manually requires several steps: setting up the interface, writing the code for generating QR codes, adding contact details, and implementing a feature that allows users to delete or edit their information. Each of these tasks requires a methodical approach, meaning the developer has to write every line of code, search for solutions when errors arise, and debug issues manually. This process, while manageable, is time-consuming. For instance, when adding the delete button, the developer might need to adjust padding, check the layout, and then test the functionality. Even for experienced coders, this takes significant time and effort, especially if they run into problems along the way that require looking up documentation or troubleshooting errors.

Now, let's consider the second version of the app, built using Cursor AI. With Cursor AI, the coding process becomes more collaborative, with the AI taking on many of the repetitive or tedious tasks. For example, instead of manually coding the delete button and adjusting its padding, the developer can simply highlight the code and use the Control K function. By typing a command like "add more padding to this button," Cursor AI instantly makes the adjustment. The developer doesn't need to worry about finding the right CSS or layout configurations because the AI handles it in seconds.

The real game-changer, however, comes when more complex changes are needed. With Cursor AI's Control L function, the developer can open the chat window and describe the desired changes in a conversational manner. For example, they can ask the AI to shift the QR code to the left side of the screen, move the contact details to the right, and replace the delete button with a menu icon. The AI processes these requests, references the entire codebase, and makes the necessary adjustments. What would have taken significant time in the manual approach is now done in minutes. Additionally, if any issues arise—such as the menu not disappearing after clicking away—the developer can simply instruct the AI to fix it, and the problem is resolved quickly.

Building the app with Cursor AI doesn't just save time; it also reduces the cognitive load on the developer. Instead of getting bogged down by minor details or troubleshooting, they can focus on the broader design and functionality of the app. Cursor AI takes care of the code structure, suggests improvements, and fixes errors as they arise, allowing the developer to move forward without the typical interruptions that slow down traditional development.

In terms of actual numbers, the difference in speed is striking. Developers using Cursor AI have reported being up to 2.5 times faster compared to when they code manually. This means that tasks that once took hours—like building and refining features, troubleshooting bugs, or adjusting layouts—can now be completed in a fraction of the time. In the case of our QR contact app, the developer using Cursor AI could have it up and running, fully tested, and refined in just a couple of hours, while the manual approach might take a full day or more, depending on the complexity of the features and any issues encountered.

In essence, the comparison between building an app manually and with Cursor AI underscores the efficiency of AI-assisted development. Cursor AI isn't just a tool for faster coding; it's a partner that makes the development process smoother and more efficient, allowing developers to accomplish more in less time. The shift in focus from writing code line by line to supervising and refining AI-generated suggestions represents a new era in coding, one where developers can maximize their output without sacrificing quality.

Iterating Code with AI: Iterating code with the help of AI in Cursor is not only a faster way to implement new features, but it also allows developers to focus on the higher-level aspects of their projects without getting stuck in the minutiae. A perfect example of this is adding a feature like profile pictures to an app. With Cursor AI, you can integrate such functionality swiftly while continuously improving the user interface through intelligent, AI-powered suggestions.

Let's say we're building a contact-sharing app, and now we want to add a feature that allows users to upload and display profile pictures alongside their contact information. Manually, this process involves multiple steps: creating the front-end interface to handle the file upload, ensuring the back-end supports storing and retrieving images, validating the file type and size, and updating the user interface to properly display the profile picture. These tasks can be labor-intensive, especially if they involve unfamiliar frameworks or require extensive testing to ensure everything works as intended.

With Cursor AI, these steps become streamlined. To begin, the developer can initiate the process by describing what they want to accomplish in the AI chat window. For instance, they might type: "I want to add an option for users to upload profile pictures with their contact cards." Cursor AI understands this request and starts generating the necessary code to implement the feature. It automatically considers all the steps needed, such as updating the user interface to include an image upload button, handling the file submission, and making sure the image is stored correctly on the server.

As the AI suggests changes, the developer can review and refine the code in real time. For example, after the initial setup is done, the AI might propose a layout for how the profile picture should appear next to the contact details. If the developer wants to make adjustments—like moving the picture to a different position or resizing it—they can simply type those instructions in the chat window. For instance, they could say, "Move the profile picture to the left and reduce its size by 20%." The AI will immediately apply the changes, and the developer can see the results in the interface.

Moreover, if any issues arise during testing, the AI can iterate on the code based on feedback. Let's say that after adding the profile picture, the developer notices that the image doesn't display properly when the contact card is first loaded. Instead of manually debugging the issue, the developer can instruct the AI to fix it. They might say, "Make sure the profile picture displays correctly when the contact card is loaded." The AI will then examine the relevant files, correct any errors, and adjust the code to ensure the image renders as expected.

This iterative process also allows for further enhancements to the user interface. For instance, the developer might want to add a fallback image for contacts who haven't uploaded a profile picture yet. They can simply ask the AI, "Add a default image for contacts without profile pictures." Cursor will generate the appropriate code, update the interface, and ensure the app functions as intended. This continuous dialogue between the developer and the AI significantly reduces the time it takes to implement, test, and refine new features.

Another layer of efficiency comes from Cursor AI's ability to reference the entire codebase. For a feature like profile picture uploads, multiple files need to be adjusted—front-end components for the user interface, back-end files for storing the images, and middleware for validation and security checks. Cursor AI manages all of this in one go. The developer doesn't have to manually track down each file or worry about forgetting a critical step. For instance, Cursor can handle file size validation, ensuring users aren't uploading unnecessarily large images, or even checking the file type to prevent unsupported formats from being uploaded.

Throughout this process, Cursor AI's ability to "remember" the changes you've asked for helps maintain consistency across the codebase. If the developer iterates on the design several times, asking for adjustments to the profile picture's size, position, or behavior, the AI ensures that each adjustment builds upon the previous one. This means you don't lose track of what's been changed, and the overall design remains coherent.

In traditional coding workflows, these kinds of changes would involve significant manual labor—writing the new functionality, testing it, tweaking the design, fixing bugs, and going back and forth between different files and functions. With Cursor AI, the iterative process becomes more fluid, as the AI handles much of the repetitive work. This allows developers to spend less time on tedious details and more time on refining the feature or adding other important functionalities.

Adding new features like profile pictures or enhancing the user interface becomes a collaborative process between the developer and the AI. The AI handles the grunt work—writing code, testing, and making adjustments—while the developer provides direction, fine-tunes the results, and focuses on the overall user experience. This kind of synergy between human input and machine learning is what makes Cursor AI so powerful, allowing developers to iterate quickly and efficiently, improving both the functionality and design of their projects without the typical headaches of manual coding.

Handling Errors and Fine-Tuning: When it comes to handling errors and fine-tuning code,

Cursor AI truly shines as a powerful tool for developers. Traditionally, debugging and troubleshooting are some of the most time-consuming aspects of coding, often requiring developers to sift through pages of code, track down the source of the issue, and manually test potential fixes. With Cursor AI, this process becomes far more streamlined, as the AI can quickly identify, troubleshoot, and iterate based on user feedback, making coding both more efficient and less error-prone.

Imagine working on a feature where, after making significant changes, you notice an error. For example, you've just implemented a profile picture upload feature for your app, but when you attempt to upload an image, the process fails, or the image doesn't display correctly. Normally, you'd need to go back and carefully examine the relevant sections of the code, isolate the issue, and then test different solutions. With Cursor AI, this process is dramatically simplified.

As soon as you encounter an issue, you can describe the problem to Cursor AI in the chat window. For instance, you might say, "The profile picture isn't displaying correctly after uploading. Can you help fix this?" The AI immediately analyzes the code and suggests potential fixes based on its understanding of your project. It doesn't just address the single file you're working on—it references the entire codebase to ensure the fix works across all necessary components, reducing the risk of introducing new bugs in other areas.

Cursor AI also allows for iterative troubleshooting. Let's say you apply the AI's suggested fix, but it doesn't fully resolve the issue. You might still notice that the image loads slowly or that it doesn't resize correctly. Instead of manually hunting down the next problem, you can continue the conversation with the AI. Simply provide additional feedback, such as, "The image is loading, but it's too slow. Can we optimize this?" The AI will then take your feedback and refine the code accordingly, optimizing the image loading process or adjusting the parameters to enhance performance.

This iterative process is where Cursor AI's real strength lies. The AI doesn't just make a one-time fix—it engages in a back-and-forth interaction with the developer, gradually improving the code based on feedback. If the issue requires multiple steps to fix, such as altering the front-end code to handle images more efficiently while also updating the back-end to improve the file upload process,

Cursor AI can manage these simultaneous changes. It provides fixes that take the broader project into account, ensuring everything stays aligned with the overall structure of the codebase.

Another key advantage of using AI for troubleshooting is its ability to catch errors that developers might miss, especially in large, complex projects. For example, Cursor AI can automatically check for inconsistencies in the code, such as mismatched data types or improper variable handling. If an error is causing an issue across multiple files, the AI can quickly scan the entire codebase, identify the problem, and suggest a fix that addresses it comprehensively. This level of insight is invaluable in preventing small errors from snowballing into larger issues that might be harder to resolve later.

Cursor AI also enhances the fine-tuning process, which is crucial when polishing a project for production. Suppose your app's new profile picture feature works, but the design looks off—perhaps the image is not properly aligned, or the padding isn't quite right. Instead of manually adjusting the styling and rechecking the layout, you can ask the AI to make those adjustments for you. For example, a simple command like "Align the profile picture to the center and adjust the padding" will prompt the AI to apply the necessary changes. If the first adjustment isn't perfect, you can iterate by providing more specific feedback, such as "Reduce the padding by 10 pixels and ensure the image is fully responsive."

This iterative cycle of refinement is what makes Cursor AI so effective. You're no longer stuck in a repetitive loop of trial and error, making one small change at a time and testing the results manually. Instead, the AI takes care of the tedious work, allowing you to focus on the bigger picture and make higher-level decisions. Each round of feedback you provide helps the AI further fine-tune the code, improving both functionality and design in a way that feels seamless and intuitive.

One of the most significant benefits of using Cursor AI for error handling and fine-tuning is that it frees developers from the burden of managing every single detail. Whether you're dealing with a bug that's hard to trace or making subtle UI adjustments, the AI can assist in real-time, solving problems as they arise while maintaining the overall structure and integrity of your codebase. This continuous interaction between the developer and the AI transforms coding from a solitary, detail-oriented task into a more collaborative process, with the AI serving as an intelligent assistant that helps troubleshoot and fine-tune on the go.

Ultimately, Cursor AI's ability to handle errors and refine code based on user feedback accelerates the development process, making it more efficient and less stressful. You can focus on building and improving your project, while the AI ensures that any issues are addressed quickly and effectively, allowing you to deliver high-quality, polished code faster than ever before.

Chapter 4: Advanced Features of Cursor AI

Command L: AI-Assisted Feature Additions: Using Cursor AI's Command L function opens up a world of possibilities when it comes to adding complex features to your project. Unlike Control K, which focuses on small, targeted adjustments, Command L engages the AI in a more conversational and comprehensive way, allowing you to tackle larger tasks that require multiple changes across your codebase. This feature is particularly useful when you're implementing more intricate functionalities, such as adding menu icons, handling user interactions like click-away functionality, or introducing completely new components. Let's walk through how AI can help streamline these processes and enhance your app's functionality with real-world examples.

Imagine you're building an app that includes user contact cards, and you want to add a menu icon next to each card. The menu will allow users to access options like editing, deleting, or sharing the contact information. In a traditional development process, you would need to create the icon, code the menu logic, and make sure it behaves correctly when users interact with it, such as clicking to open or clicking away to close the menu. Each of these steps requires careful attention to detail and can be time-consuming.

With Command L, you can dramatically simplify this process. Start by opening the chat window with Control L and describe what you want to achieve. For instance, you might say, "Add a menu icon to the contact card that opens on click, with options to edit, delete, or share, and close when clicking away." Cursor AI instantly processes your request, taking into account the relevant parts of your codebase that it has already indexed. This context-awareness allows the AI to suggest changes that seamlessly integrate with your existing components.

The AI might first suggest adding a standard menu icon—often represented by three vertical dots. Cursor will not only create the visual icon but also generate the necessary code to handle the menu's behavior when clicked. Once you approve the initial suggestion, the AI moves on to creating the logic for the menu items themselves, such as "Edit," "Delete," and "Share." These options are coded as clickable buttons or links, complete with the appropriate event handlers that trigger the desired actions.

One of the most impressive aspects of Command L is its ability to handle the nuances of user interaction. After the menu is functional, you can test it in the app. But what happens when a user clicks away from the menu? Ideally, the menu should close automatically to enhance the user experience. Instead of manually writing this logic, you can instruct Cursor AI to add click-away functionality. A simple prompt, such as "Add click-away functionality to close the menu when the user clicks outside of it," is all it takes. Cursor will update the code to include an event listener that detects when a user clicks outside the menu and closes it accordingly.

In real-world application, this click-away functionality enhances the app's usability, providing a smoother and more intuitive experience for users. Without the AI's assistance, implementing this feature could involve significant trial and error, especially when dealing with the event handling logic that ensures the menu behaves correctly across different interactions. Cursor AI eliminates much of this manual effort, enabling you to focus on refining the overall design and functionality rather than getting bogged down in small details.

Beyond simple menus, Command L is also adept at handling more complex, multi-file changes. Let's say you want to introduce an image upload feature to the contact card, allowing users to add profile pictures. This process involves not only updating the front-end user interface but also modifying the back-end logic to handle file uploads and storing images securely. Describing this in the chat window, you might say, "Add an image upload feature to the contact card, store the image in a cloud bucket, and display the uploaded image on the card."

Cursor AI understands that this request involves multiple components. It will first create an upload button on the contact card, then write the necessary back-end logic to handle the image upload. The AI can generate code that integrates with cloud storage services—such as Google Cloud or AWS S3—to securely store the image files. After the image is uploaded, the AI ensures that the file path is linked to the contact card so the profile picture is displayed correctly in the app's interface.

When dealing with features that span multiple files—like adding an image upload system—the AI becomes even more valuable. It doesn't just change one part of the code and leave the rest up to you; it ensures that all the necessary files are updated in sync. For example, it might generate changes to the back-end API, ensuring the image data is passed correctly to the database. Simultaneously, it could modify the front-end to properly render the uploaded image, all while maintaining a cohesive structure across the codebase.

Once the image upload feature is implemented, you can further refine it using the iterative power of Command L. If, after testing, you realize that the uploaded image is too large or isn't properly aligned, you can ask the AI to make adjustments. A prompt like "Resize the uploaded image to fit within a 150x150 pixel container" or "Center the profile picture on the contact card" will prompt Cursor to adjust the layout and styling, ensuring that the feature integrates smoothly with the rest of the app's design.

This kind of back-and-forth collaboration with the AI reduces the complexity and frustration often associated with building complex features from scratch. Instead of manually writing and testing each piece of functionality, you can rely on the AI to handle much of the heavy lifting, only stepping in when you need to provide high-level direction or fine-tune the details.

Overall, Command L transforms how developers approach feature additions, making it faster and more intuitive to implement complex functionality. Whether you're adding interactive menus, handling user interactions like click-away events, or integrating multi-file systems like image uploads, Cursor AI ensures that the process is smooth, efficient, and error-free. By acting as an intelligent assistant, Cursor allows you to focus on the creative aspects of development, while the AI handles the technical intricacies, enabling faster and smarter coding.

Multi-File Requests: When working on a complex application, implementing new features often requires modifying multiple files simultaneously—especially when adding elements like image uploads or setting up database connections. Traditionally, this would involve manually navigating through different parts of your project, ensuring that changes are consistent across all relevant files. With Cursor AI, however, multi-file requests become significantly easier, as the AI can reference and modify various parts of the codebase at once, ensuring a seamless integration of new features without having to tediously manage each file.

Let's take the example of adding an image upload feature to your app, which requires front-end, back-end, and database changes. Normally, you'd need to adjust your front-end user interface to handle the upload input, set up middleware to process the file, and modify the back-end code to store the image in a cloud bucket or database. Additionally, you'd have to write logic to fetch and display the uploaded image whenever a user views the contact card. Cursor AI simplifies this process through its ability to handle multi-file requests, taking care of the complex task of managing all these components together.

To begin, you'd describe your goal to Cursor AI in the chat window using a prompt like, "Add an image upload feature for the contact card, store the image in Google Cloud Storage, and display it on the card." The AI processes this request by referencing all necessary files in your codebase. This is where Cursor's codebase indexing feature shines—since the AI has a holistic view of your entire project, it knows which files need to be modified and how they interact with each other.

The first step involves updating the front-end. Cursor will generate code to create a button that allows users to select an image from their device.

This typically involves adding an input field to handle file selection, along with some basic validation to ensure the file is an appropriate type and size. Simultaneously, the AI writes the logic to handle this input in the form of a front-end component that passes the image data to the back-end for processing.

On the back-end, things get a bit more complex, but this is where Cursor AI excels at handling multi-file updates. The AI will recognize that the image needs to be uploaded to a cloud storage service, such as Google Cloud or AWS S3, and it will generate the necessary server-side logic to accomplish this. It writes code to securely transmit the image file to the cloud bucket, validate its format, and ensure it doesn't exceed a specific size limit. Additionally, Cursor will modify your environment configuration files to include any necessary credentials or API keys for the cloud storage service, making sure that the integration is secure and scalable.

At the same time, the AI updates the database logic to store the image's URL once it has been uploaded. This is crucial for retrieving the image later when displaying the user's profile picture. Cursor AI will automatically modify your database schema if needed, adding a new field to store the URL or updating existing tables to accommodate the image data. It ensures that each file involved in managing the database—whether it's the model, controller, or API route—is updated in sync so that everything runs smoothly when the image upload is triggered.

What makes Cursor particularly powerful in these multi-file scenarios is its ability to test and validate the changes it makes. Once the initial code is generated, you can test the feature by attempting to upload an image. If any issues arise—such as the image not displaying correctly or an error with the cloud storage—the AI can quickly iterate based on your feedback. You might encounter a problem where the image uploads but isn't properly saved to the database, or maybe the image is too large to render properly on the contact card. Instead of manually searching for the issue across multiple files, you can simply tell the AI, "The image isn't saving correctly—can you check the database connection?" The AI will identify the problem, update the code as needed, and ensure that the feature works as intended.

Once the back-end and database logic is complete, Cursor AI ensures that the front-end is properly set up to display the uploaded image. This involves retrieving the image's URL from the database and rendering it in the user interface. The AI will handle this automatically by updating the relevant files responsible for rendering the contact card. You can further refine the layout by asking Cursor to adjust how the image appears—for example, "Resize the image to fit within a 150x150 pixel container on the contact card." The AI will make the necessary changes to the CSS or styling components, ensuring the profile picture displays correctly across different devices and screen sizes.

In addition to handling the front-end, back-end, and database updates, Cursor AI also considers the middleware that might be needed for processing and validating the image. For example, if the image upload needs to be filtered through a security layer to check for malicious content, Cursor can automatically integrate these checks into the code. It ensures that every part of the process—from file selection to storage and display—is secure and optimized, with no steps left out.

Multi-file requests like this demonstrate the real power of Cursor AI: the ability to coordinate complex changes across different parts of a project without the developer having to manually manage each file. Cursor eliminates the repetitive, error-prone nature of switching between files and ensures that everything is updated in sync, saving hours of manual coding and debugging. The AI not only generates the code but also keeps track of how all the different components interact, allowing you to focus on refining the feature or improving other areas of the project.

By simplifying multi-file changes—whether for image uploads, database connections, or other complex features—Cursor AI transforms the development process, allowing you to move quickly and confidently as you implement new features across your entire codebase.

Composer Feature in Beta: The Composer feature in Cursor AI is an exciting addition currently in its beta phase, designed to handle large, multi-file changes with even greater efficiency. For developers working on complex projects, where adding new features or refactoring existing ones requires coordinating updates across numerous files, the Composer is a powerful tool. It aims to streamline these large-scale changes by allowing Cursor to work on multiple files in parallel, making the development process faster and more organized. However, as a feature still in beta, it comes with certain limitations that developers should be aware of when using it.

At its core, the Composer is intended to help manage situations where single-file edits aren't enough—such as when you're implementing a new feature that affects multiple layers of the project, from front-end components to back-end logic and database schemas. Traditionally, developers would need to navigate between various files, making sure that changes in one file are reflected correctly in others, often leading to long and error-prone coding sessions. The Composer simplifies this by allowing Cursor AI to make all the necessary changes simultaneously across the codebase.

Let's consider an example where you're refactoring a major part of your project. Suppose you've written a large file that contains several different functions and components, and you now want to break it down into smaller, more manageable pieces by creating separate files for each function or component. Without the Composer, this would be a labor-intensive process, requiring you to move code between files, update references, and ensure that everything still works as expected. With the Composer, however, you can issue a single request, such as, "Refactor this file into separate files for each component," and Cursor AI will handle the rest. It moves the relevant code into new files, updates the import/export statements, and makes sure all references across the project remain intact.

The parallel processing capabilities of the Composer make it particularly useful for large projects where multiple files need to be created, modified, or refactored in one go. By working on these files simultaneously, the Composer significantly reduces the time it takes to implement such changes, allowing you to keep the focus on high-level decisions rather than the grunt work of manually shifting code around.

However, since the Composer is still in beta, there are some limitations to be mindful of. First, while it works well for managing straightforward changes across multiple files, it can sometimes struggle with more complex dependencies or project structures. For instance, if the project contains deeply nested files or intricate relationships between different components, the Composer might not always accurately track all the connections, which could result in missing references or incorrect file structures. In these cases, the AI may attempt to refactor files in a way that leaves behind broken links or dependencies that still need to be manually fixed.

Additionally, because the Composer handles changes in parallel, there's a chance that small mistakes can propagate across multiple files, making it harder to identify and fix the root cause. For example, if the AI misunderstands a variable reference or doesn't properly update an import path, the error can affect every file that relies on that reference, creating a cascade of issues. While the feature is designed to speed up large changes, this limitation means that developers should still review the results carefully, especially in complex projects.

Another limitation is that the Composer, due to its current beta status, may not always offer the same level of detailed control that developers might need for highly specific tasks. When dealing with large refactoring jobs or significant feature additions, the scope of changes might be too broad for the AI to handle perfectly. For example, if the AI is tasked with reorganizing an entire module or refactoring deeply intertwined code, it might not capture all the nuances of the project, leading to inconsistencies or gaps that need to be manually resolved.

Despite these limitations, the Composer shows tremendous potential. As it evolves beyond its beta stage, it is likely to become a go-to feature for developers managing large-scale projects that require frequent multi-file updates or refactoring. Its ability to handle multiple files in parallel saves a great deal of time, and once refined, it promises to provide even more accuracy and control in making sweeping changes across a codebase.

The real strength of the Composer lies in its vision: automating large, cumbersome tasks that would otherwise take developers hours or even days to complete manually. By reducing the overhead associated with managing dozens of interconnected files, it allows developers to focus on more creative and complex aspects of their projects, while Cursor AI takes care of the behind-the-scenes organization and code structure.

In its current form, the Composer is an incredibly useful tool for managing less intricate multi-file changes—such as splitting up large files, refactoring straightforward components, or making structural improvements across several files. However, for more complex or deeply nested codebases, developers will need to proceed with caution, using the Composer as a starting point but being prepared to manually review and tweak the results.

As Cursor AI continues to develop the Composer, addressing its current limitations and refining its ability to handle more complex tasks, it will likely become an indispensable feature for developers working on large-scale projects. In the meantime, it remains a valuable tool for managing multi-file requests, particularly when time and efficiency are critical, but with the understanding that it's still a work in progress.

Chapter 5: Enhancing User Experience with Design and Automation

Incorporating User Feedback for UI Adjustments: Incorporating user feedback into the user interface (UI) is a critical part of development, as it directly impacts the usability and overall experience of an application. With Cursor AI, making real-time adjustments based on user feedback becomes a faster, more fluid process. Instead of diving into the code to manually tweak layout, spacing, or element positioning, you can use AI to efficiently modify the UI based on feedback, ensuring that the changes are implemented quickly and correctly. Cursor AI's ability to respond to design requests and refine elements helps developers perfect their interfaces with minimal effort.

Let's consider a common scenario where users provide feedback on image placement in your app. For instance, after introducing a feature that allows users to upload profile pictures, you might receive feedback that the images are too large or aren't properly aligned with other elements on the page. Manually adjusting the size and alignment could involve combing through CSS or style files, tweaking values, and then testing repeatedly. With Cursor AI, however, these changes can be implemented in just a few steps.

To start, you can describe the feedback directly to Cursor in the chat window. Let's say users have mentioned that the profile picture should be smaller and aligned to the left of the contact card. You can simply type, "Resize the profile picture to 100x100 pixels and align it to the left side of the contact card." Cursor AI will instantly generate the required CSS or style modifications, adjusting the image size and position accordingly. The AI handles the heavy lifting, applying the changes across all necessary files so you don't need to manually track down where the style is defined.

Once the adjustments are made, testing the new layout is as easy as refreshing the app to see the updated UI. If the initial change still doesn't quite meet user expectations—perhaps the image is now aligned but looks slightly off-center relative to the text—you can provide additional feedback to Cursor AI. A follow-up instruction like, "Add 10 pixels of padding between the profile picture and the text," will prompt Cursor to refine the layout further. The AI iterates based on your input, continuing to adjust the elements until they match the desired look and feel.

This process also extends to more complex UI elements. Let's say users have suggested that the app's navigation menu should be more intuitive, with clearer separation between clickable buttons. Instead of diving deep into your codebase to adjust each button's padding and margin, you can rely on Cursor AI to handle it for you. By typing something like, "Increase the padding between navigation buttons and make the font size larger," the AI will automatically update the relevant style rules, increasing the padding and adjusting the font size of the buttons for better usability.

In addition to layout adjustments, Cursor AI can handle visual refinements, such as color changes and hover effects. For example, if users report that certain buttons are hard to distinguish from the background color, you can instruct the AI to fix this by saying, "Change the button background color to blue and add a hover effect that makes the text bold." Cursor will generate the necessary CSS to adjust the button's background color and add the hover effect, ensuring that the design is both functional and visually appealing. These changes are implemented in seconds, allowing you to immediately test them and gather further feedback if necessary.

Another area where Cursor AI shines is in handling responsiveness. User feedback might indicate that the UI looks great on desktops but becomes cluttered or misaligned on smaller devices. Instead of manually writing media queries and adjusting every responsive breakpoint, you can instruct Cursor AI to make the necessary changes. For example, "Make the profile picture responsive, scaling down to 75x75 pixels on screens smaller than 600 pixels," allows the AI to handle the layout adjustments for different screen sizes. The AI will generate the appropriate CSS, ensuring that the image remains well-proportioned and properly aligned regardless of the device being used.

Cursor AI's ability to incorporate user feedback doesn't stop at visual adjustments. It can also handle interactive elements like buttons or menus. Suppose users report that clicking on a menu icon doesn't feel responsive enough, or the dropdown menu is too slow to appear. You can ask the AI to improve the interaction by saying, "Speed up the dropdown menu animation and make it appear instantly on hover." Cursor will adjust the timing and behavior of the animation, improving the user experience without you needing to dive into JavaScript or CSS animations manually.

The iterative nature of Cursor AI makes it ideal for incorporating ongoing feedback. As users interact with the app and offer suggestions, you can continuously refine the UI without going through lengthy cycles of manual adjustments, testing, and reworking. Cursor's intelligent suggestions keep the development process agile, allowing for quick refinements that respond to user needs in real time. Moreover, since the AI has access to the entire codebase, it ensures that each adjustment is consistent across all files, so the changes you implement in one part of the project don't inadvertently break something elsewhere.

Overall, Cursor AI's ability to handle UI adjustments based on feedback allows for a more responsive and efficient development process. Whether it's fine-tuning image placement, adjusting layout, enhancing button interactions, or improving responsiveness, the AI acts as a powerful tool to perfect the user interface without the usual time-consuming back-and-forth between coding and testing. This frees developers to focus on bigger design decisions, knowing that Cursor can take care of the details, ensuring that the app remains polished, user-friendly, and visually appealing.

Automating Refactoring: Refactoring is an essential process in software development, aimed at improving the structure, readability, and maintainability of code without changing its external behavior. Over time, as projects grow and new features are added, the codebase can become cluttered or hard to manage. This makes refactoring necessary to keep the project maintainable and efficient. Traditionally, refactoring can be a time-consuming and painstaking task, but with Cursor AI, this process becomes significantly easier, faster, and more effective.

Cursor AI is a valuable tool when it comes to automating the refactoring of messy code. Its built-in understanding of best practices, combined with its ability to navigate through an entire codebase, allows it to identify areas that can be improved and suggest changes that enhance the structure and readability of the code. Whether it's breaking down large functions, simplifying complex logic, or removing redundant code, Cursor AI streamlines the refactoring process, making it more efficient.

Let's explore how Cursor AI can be used to clean up a codebase and make it more maintainable.

Breaking Down Large Functions

One of the most common refactoring tasks is breaking down large, monolithic functions into smaller, more manageable pieces. Large functions tend to be difficult to read, test, and maintain because they often contain multiple responsibilities and complex logic. With Cursor AI, refactoring these functions is as simple as issuing a command.

For example, if you have a large function that handles multiple tasks, such as user authentication, data validation, and API calls, you can ask Cursor to refactor it. You might start by saying, "Refactor this function to separate user authentication, data validation, and API calls into different functions." Cursor AI will analyze the function and automatically extract the relevant code into separate, well-named functions. The AI ensures that each new function performs a single responsibility, which adheres to the Single

Responsibility Principle—a core tenet of clean code.

After the refactoring, your code becomes more modular, easier to test, and more maintainable. Each function can now be modified independently without affecting the rest of the code, which reduces the risk of introducing bugs during future updates or feature additions.

Simplifying Complex Logic

Complex conditional statements or deeply nested loops can make code difficult to understand and maintain. Cursor AI can help simplify these structures by identifying patterns that can be refactored into more concise and readable forms.

Imagine you have a function with a series of deeply nested `if-else` statements. This type of logic is not only hard to read but also prone to errors as conditions become more complex. By asking Cursor to refactor the function, the AI can simplify the logic by converting the `if-else` statements into a switch-case structure or by replacing them with early returns or guard clauses where appropriate. A simple instruction like, "Refactor the nested if-else statements to make the logic cleaner," prompts the AI to reorganize the code, making it easier to follow and maintain.

Similarly, if your code contains complex loops that perform multiple tasks, Cursor AI can refactor them by breaking the logic into smaller, more readable pieces. This can involve moving certain operations out of the loop or even replacing loops with more efficient constructs like map or filter functions, depending on the programming language. The result is a more efficient and maintainable codebase, with clearer logic and reduced complexity.

Removing Redundant Code

As projects evolve, codebases often accumulate redundant or duplicate code. This can happen when developers copy and paste code across different parts of the project or when old logic remains even after it's no longer needed. Cursor AI can help identify and eliminate this redundancy, improving the overall cleanliness of the code.

For example, let's say you have two functions that perform similar tasks but have slight variations. Instead of keeping both functions, which increases the risk of bugs and inconsistencies, you can instruct Cursor to refactor the code by consolidating the duplicate logic into a single reusable function. By saying,

"Remove redundant code and consolidate similar functions," the AI will analyze the code, merge the duplicate logic, and ensure that the single function can handle the necessary variations through parameters or conditional checks.

This process not only reduces the overall size of the codebase but also makes it easier to maintain, as you no longer have to update multiple sections of code when making changes. Cursor AI's ability to spot redundancy and clean it up ensures that your project remains lean and efficient.

Enhancing Code Readability

Readable code is maintainable code. One of the goals of refactoring is to improve the readability of code by making it more intuitive for developers to understand. Cursor AI excels at this by automatically renaming variables, functions, and classes to more descriptive names based on their purpose.

For instance, if your project contains variables or functions with generic names like `data1`, `process`, or `doStuff`, you can ask Cursor to rename them to something more meaningful. You might instruct the AI with a command like, "Rename variables and functions to be more descriptive," and the AI will suggest new names based on the code's context. This simple change makes the code easier to follow, reducing the cognitive load on developers who need to work on the project in the future.

Cursor can also help organize code by applying consistent formatting across the entire codebase. If your project suffers from inconsistent indentation, spacing, or code styles, you can ask the AI to automatically format the code according to industry-standard practices or your team's preferred style guide. This uniformity makes the code easier to navigate and contributes to a more professional, maintainable project.

Refactoring Across Multiple Files

For larger projects, refactoring often involves changes that span multiple files. This can be particularly challenging when functions or classes are used in different parts of the project. Cursor AI's ability to index the entire codebase allows it to track dependencies across multiple files and refactor them in a consistent way.

For example, if you need to rename a function or refactor a class that is used in several parts of the project, Cursor AI can make the necessary changes across all files at once. You can ask the AI to "Refactor this function across the entire project," and it will ensure that every reference to that function is updated in line with the new changes. This eliminates the need for manual updates and reduces the chance of introducing errors or breaking functionality.

By handling these multi-file refactoring tasks, Cursor AI ensures that your codebase remains consistent and up-to-date, without the typical risks associated with large-scale changes.

Conclusion

Automating refactoring with Cursor AI not only saves time but also ensures that your codebase stays clean, efficient, and maintainable. By breaking down large functions, simplifying complex logic, removing redundant code, and improving readability, Cursor AI helps you maintain a high-quality codebase that's easy to work with. Its ability to handle refactoring across multiple files further enhances its value, especially for large projects that require consistent updates throughout. In short, Cursor AI transforms what is often a tedious and manual process into a streamlined, automated workflow, allowing you to focus on building and improving your project with confidence.

Using Screenshots to Code Designs: One of the most exciting and innovative features of Cursor AI is its ability to convert visual designs, such as screenshots or Figma files, directly into working code. This capability revolutionizes the design-to-code workflow, significantly reducing the manual effort required to translate a static design into functional code. For developers, this means faster implementation of user interfaces, fewer chances of human error, and a more streamlined process for turning ideas into reality. Whether you're handed a design mockup or a rough sketch, Cursor AI can help bridge the gap between design and development with remarkable efficiency.

Imagine you've received a set of design mockups from your UI/UX team, perhaps in the form of Figma files or even simple screenshots. The designs detail a new layout for your app's user profile page, featuring images, text fields, buttons, and an interactive menu. Normally, you'd have to carefully examine each part of the design, write the corresponding HTML, CSS, and JavaScript, and then iterate multiple times to ensure that the code matches the design's pixel-perfect precision. This manual process can be time-consuming, often requiring a lot of back-and-forth to ensure everything looks exactly as it should.

With Cursor AI, this tedious process becomes much more fluid. Instead of manually coding each design element, you can take a screenshot of the design or export the Figma file, and then feed it into Cursor. By simply opening the chat window and giving the AI instructions such as, "Generate the code for this design from the screenshot," Cursor AI will analyze the visual elements and begin generating the corresponding HTML, CSS, and even JavaScript if necessary. This instant translation from design to code drastically cuts down the time it takes to get from concept to working product.

For example, let's say the design includes a profile picture with a rounded border, a user name displayed next to it, and a few interactive buttons for actions like editing the profile or sending a message. Cursor AI can identify these elements from the screenshot and generate the

HTML and CSS needed to render the profile picture with the appropriate styling (such as the border radius to make the image round), along with the layout for the name and buttons. What used to take several manual steps is now condensed into a few moments of interaction with the AI.

The beauty of this feature lies in its adaptability. If the generated code doesn't align perfectly with your design specifications, you can easily instruct Cursor to make adjustments. For instance, if the profile picture is too large or the buttons aren't spaced correctly, you can say, "Resize the profile picture to 150x150 pixels and add 20 pixels of margin between the buttons." Cursor AI will update the code accordingly, refining the layout until it matches the design exactly. This back-and-forth interaction allows for quick iteration, ensuring that your design vision is realized without needing to write each line of code manually.

Moreover, Cursor AI's ability to interpret design elements goes beyond simple static images. If the design includes interactive components—such as dropdown menus, sliders, or hover effects—Cursor can generate the JavaScript necessary to bring these features to life. For example, if the design mockup includes a dropdown menu that should appear when a user hovers over an icon, Cursor will not only generate the HTML and CSS for the menu but also write the JavaScript to handle the hover interaction. You can further refine this interaction by giving feedback, such as, "Make the dropdown appear with a fade-in animation," and Cursor AI will make the required changes to the code.

Another advantage of using Cursor AI for converting designs into code is its ability to handle responsive layouts. Often, designs are created for desktop screens, but the application needs to work across a range of devices, including tablets and smartphones. Instead of manually writing media queries and testing how each element behaves at different screen sizes, you can instruct Cursor AI to automatically generate responsive code. For instance, you might say, "Make the profile page responsive, ensuring the layout adjusts for mobile screens under 600 pixels wide." Cursor will analyze the design and generate the appropriate media queries and CSS to ensure that the layout remains consistent across devices.

This functionality extends to more complex design features as well. Suppose your design includes a grid of images that needs to adapt to different screen sizes, showing more images per row on larger screens and fewer on smaller screens. With Cursor AI, you can easily convert this design into a responsive grid layout. You might instruct the AI with a command like, "Create a responsive grid that shows four images per row on desktop and two per row on mobile." The AI will generate the necessary CSS grid or flexbox code, ensuring the design scales smoothly based on the screen size.

The ability to convert screenshots or Figma files into working code through Cursor AI doesn't just save time—it also enhances accuracy. In manual processes, small discrepancies often arise between the design and the final implementation, whether it's a slight difference in font size, padding, or color. By using AI to interpret the design and generate the code, you eliminate many of these inconsistencies, ensuring that the final product matches the design as closely as possible.

Of course, the process doesn't end once the code is generated. Cursor AI allows for continuous iteration and refinement. As feedback comes in from designers or users, you can quickly update the code to reflect new changes. Whether it's adjusting the placement of an image, tweaking the color scheme, or adding new interactive features, Cursor AI enables you to make these updates effortlessly. Simply describe the changes, and the AI will modify the code accordingly, keeping the development process agile and responsive to evolving design needs.

In summary, Cursor AI's ability to convert visual designs into functional code significantly reduces the manual effort involved in design-to-code transitions. By analyzing screenshots or Figma files and generating the corresponding HTML, CSS, and JavaScript, the AI accelerates the process of implementing user interfaces, making it easier to create pixel-perfect designs with minimal manual intervention. This not only speeds up development but also ensures a higher level of accuracy, as the AI works to faithfully reproduce the design in code, with the added flexibility of making iterative adjustments based on user or designer feedback. The result is a more efficient, streamlined workflow that allows developers to focus on higher-level decisions while letting the AI handle the details of turning design into reality.

Chapter 6: Troubleshooting and Debugging with Cursor AI

When it comes to troubleshooting and debugging, Cursor AI shines as an invaluable tool for developers. Traditionally, debugging requires extensive manual investigation—locating the source of an error, testing various solutions, and running through cycles of trial and error. Cursor AI streamlines this process, allowing developers to tackle issues in real-time by offering intelligent suggestions as soon as problems arise. Whether you're dealing with minor bugs in your front-end code or complex back-end issues like database connection failures, Cursor AI's ability to pinpoint and fix errors significantly accelerates the debugging process.

Real-time debugging is one of the key areas where Cursor AI truly stands out. Imagine you're working on a feature, and as you test the app, you notice an unexpected error. Perhaps a button isn't working as intended or a function isn't returning the correct value. With traditional debugging, you'd manually trace through your code, searching for the root cause, potentially spending hours fixing something that seems minor. With Cursor AI, you can simply describe the issue in the chat window. For instance, you might say, "The button isn't triggering the correct function when clicked." In response, Cursor AI quickly analyzes the code and highlights the section responsible for the error.

By understanding the context of your project, Cursor AI can suggest specific fixes. It doesn't just identify that there's an issue; it offers a solution based on its analysis. If the problem lies in how an event handler is written or if the wrong function is being triggered, the AI will suggest modifications to fix the code. You can choose to apply the fix directly, and if the issue persists, Cursor can further refine its suggestions based on real-time feedback. This back-and-forth interaction enables a much faster debugging process compared to manually searching for and correcting errors.

One of the great strengths of Cursor AI is that it keeps track of the larger codebase, so it understands the dependencies between different files. This allows it to provide more holistic suggestions when troubleshooting. For example, if a bug in one file affects the functionality of a related file, Cursor AI can recognize this and suggest changes across both files. This eliminates the need for developers to jump between files, trying to figure out how different parts of the project interact—Cursor handles that complexity automatically.

Now let's look at a more challenging scenario: debugging a database connection issue. Managing errors with database connections can be tricky, especially when it involves handling interactions between the front-end, back-end, and the database itself. Suppose your app is trying to upload an image and store the image's URL in a database, but something goes wrong with the connection, and the image doesn't save properly. Traditionally, you'd need to manually trace the issue, checking both the front-end code that handles the upload and the back-end logic that connects to the database.

Cursor AI simplifies this process by quickly identifying the source of the error. If you notice that the image upload fails, you can describe the issue to the AI: "The image upload isn't saving the URL in the database." Cursor AI will examine the relevant sections of the codebase, including the back-end logic that processes the upload, the API that communicates with the database, and the database schema itself. It might detect that there's a mismatch between the data type expected by the database and the data being sent, or perhaps the API request isn't attaching the necessary credentials for authentication.

Once the AI identifies the problem, it suggests a fix. For instance, if the issue is that the database is expecting a string while the code is passing an object, Cursor AI will generate the code needed to convert the object into a string before sending it to the database. If the problem lies in the connection string for the database itself—such as a misconfigured environment variable—Cursor AI can guide you through correcting the configuration, ensuring that the app can successfully connect to the server.

Database interactions often involve layers of complexity, such as handling large datasets, dealing with query optimization, or managing storage limits. Cursor AI can help streamline these processes by ensuring that your database queries are written efficiently. If you're working with large tables or datasets and notice performance issues, you can ask the AI to optimize the query. For example, "Optimize this query for retrieving user data from a large database" will prompt Cursor AI to analyze the current query and suggest improvements, such as adding indexes, optimizing filters, or reducing the number of retrieved columns to improve performance.

Another common issue in back-end development is managing timeouts and handling errors when the server or database becomes unresponsive. Suppose your app is trying to query the database for a user's profile picture, but the request times out or returns an error due to network issues. Cursor AI can help manage these errors by suggesting ways to handle timeouts or implement error-handling logic. A simple request like, "Add error handling for timeouts when querying the database" will prompt Cursor to generate code that gracefully manages the timeout, retries the request if necessary, or displays an appropriate error message to the user.

Furthermore, Cursor AI can help prevent future errors by suggesting ways to improve the robustness of your code. If your app is vulnerable to issues like SQL injection attacks or if the database is not securely handling input, the AI can point out these vulnerabilities and suggest solutions to mitigate the risk. For example, Cursor might recommend parameterized queries or other security best practices to ensure your database interactions are safe from malicious input.

In summary, Cursor AI transforms the traditional debugging process by offering real-time suggestions and fixes for both front-end and back-end issues. Whether it's resolving minor UI bugs or managing complex database interactions, Cursor AI intelligently analyzes the problem and provides tailored solutions that save time and reduce frustration. Its ability to track dependencies across files and offer holistic fixes ensures that debugging is not only faster but more reliable. In the case of back-end issues, particularly related to database connections, Cursor's capability to manage server storage, optimize queries, and handle errors makes it an indispensable tool for modern development. Through intelligent suggestions and iterative problem-solving, Cursor AI allows developers to focus on building and refining their projects rather than getting stuck in the weeds of error management.

Chapter 7: The Future of AI in Coding

The future of AI in coding is poised to bring even more groundbreaking advancements, building upon the capabilities of tools like Cursor AI. As AI continues to evolve, we can expect coding tools to become more powerful, intuitive, and integrated, allowing developers to focus on higher-level problem-solving while automating much of the repetitive and labor-intensive aspects of coding. In the coming years, the role of AI in coding is set to expand in ways that will redefine how software is created, maintained, and optimized.

Beyond Cursor AI: What's Next in AI-Powered Coding Tools?

While Cursor AI has already demonstrated how AI can accelerate coding through real-time assistance, multi-file refactoring, and design-to-code automation, the next generation of AI-powered coding tools will likely take things further. One area that will see significant growth is **AI-driven code generation** that not only assists developers in writing code but can also autonomously build entire applications based on high-level specifications. Imagine a scenario where you provide a detailed description of the app's functionality and design, and the AI constructs the entire architecture, front-end, back-end, and database systems from scratch, all tailored to your specifications.

In addition to generating code, we can expect AI tools to move beyond simple syntax suggestions and delve deeper into **predictive development**. These systems will learn from patterns across vast datasets of open-source projects and private repositories, allowing them to predict potential problems before they arise. This would enable AI to flag not just immediate issues like bugs or errors but also long-term design flaws, scalability bottlenecks, or security vulnerabilities. The AI could then proactively suggest more scalable and secure architectures, making complex software systems more robust from the start.

Another exciting trend we'll see in AI coding tools is **continuous optimization**. Currently, developers must manually refactor or optimize code for performance, security, or maintainability. However, future AI systems could autonomously monitor your codebase, suggesting improvements in real-time. These AI-driven optimizations will likely go beyond mere code structure and extend to performance tuning, suggesting more efficient algorithms, database queries, or server configurations, all tailored to the specific context of your project.

Another area where AI is likely to make significant strides is in **collaborative coding environments**. Today's AI tools, like Cursor, already support real-time suggestions and code generation for individual developers. However, in the future, AI will likely play a central role in **team-based development workflows**. Imagine AI systems embedded within version control platforms like GitHub or GitLab, automatically reviewing pull requests, identifying conflicts, and resolving merge issues. These systems could autonomously manage coding standards across a large team, ensuring consistency, security, and scalability in a unified manner.

How AI Will Continue to Impact Developers

The integration of AI into coding practices will continue to reshape the developer experience, and it's crucial for developers to stay prepared for a future where AI is central to every aspect of software development. As AI tools become more sophisticated, they will handle increasingly complex tasks, pushing developers into more strategic roles where creativity, architecture, and innovation take precedence over routine coding tasks.

One of the most immediate impacts AI will have is **reducing the need for boilerplate coding**. Tasks like setting up project structures, managing APIs, or creating CRUD (Create, Read, Update, Delete) operations will become almost entirely automated. This will free developers from these repetitive tasks, allowing them to focus on solving more intricate and domain-specific problems. As a result, developers will shift from being primarily code writers to **system designers and problem**

solvers, focusing more on defining the logic and less on writing syntax.

In this future, **domain-specific AI coding tools** will become increasingly prevalent. These tools will be tailored to specialized fields such as blockchain, cybersecurity, machine learning, and game development, providing highly targeted suggestions and code snippets optimized for each domain. Developers working in niche fields will benefit from these advanced AI systems, which will help them write highly specialized code faster and with fewer errors.

Additionally, AI will enhance the **learning curve for new developers**. AI-driven tools like Cursor already assist developers by providing real-time suggestions and contextual help. In the future, these systems will evolve into **AI-powered mentors** that guide developers through complex coding challenges, suggest best practices, and offer personalized learning paths. This will make coding more accessible to a broader audience, enabling people with limited programming experience to build complex applications through AI assistance. New developers will be able to tackle larger and more ambitious projects earlier in their careers, leading to faster innovation and more creative solutions in the industry.

Another important way AI will continue to impact developers is through **increased productivity and collaboration**. As AI tools become better at managing multi-file changes, debugging complex systems, and handling large-scale refactoring, development teams will be able to work more efficiently. This will reduce the need for lengthy code reviews, manual debugging sessions, or repetitive optimization cycles. AI will serve as a powerful collaborator, handling much of the heavy lifting while enabling teams to work faster and more cohesively.

Furthermore, as AI becomes more integral to the coding process, **continuous integration and deployment (CI/CD) pipelines** will benefit from more sophisticated automation. AI systems will likely become more involved in managing deployment workflows, optimizing performance across different environments, and ensuring that software updates are secure, efficient, and bug-free. Developers will need to become adept at working alongside AI systems that manage various aspects of the software development lifecycle.

Looking ahead, **AI ethics and responsibility** will also become an essential aspect of a developer's role. As AI systems take on more responsibilities, from code generation to system optimization, developers will need to ensure that these tools are used responsibly. This includes ensuring that the AI-generated code is secure, free of bias, and complies with industry regulations. Developers will play a key role in supervising and guiding AI behavior, making ethical considerations a fundamental part of the development process.

Preparing for a More AI-Centric Future

For developers to thrive in an AI-powered future, continuous learning and adaptability will be critical. While AI will automate many routine coding tasks, developers will need to focus on enhancing their **architectural thinking, creativity, and problem-solving skills**. Understanding how to structure large systems, make high-level design decisions, and work with complex AI-driven tools will become essential skills.

Additionally, learning how to **collaborate with AI** effectively will be a key asset. This involves understanding the strengths and limitations of AI systems, knowing when to rely on AI-generated suggestions, and recognizing when human oversight is necessary. Developers who can strike the right balance between leveraging AI for efficiency and applying their human judgment to critical decision-making processes will be better positioned to succeed.

As AI becomes more embedded in coding, developers will also need to develop an understanding of **AI ethics and governance**. This includes ensuring that AI-generated code follows best practices, remains secure, and adheres to privacy and ethical standards. Developers will be responsible for supervising AI systems, guiding their decisions, and ensuring they contribute positively to both the technical and social aspects of software development.

In conclusion, the future of AI in coding promises exciting advancements that will transform how developers work. Tools like Cursor AI are just the beginning, as future AI-powered coding systems will take on even more complex tasks, from generating full applications to managing team-based workflows. Developers must stay ahead by embracing continuous learning, honing their creative problem-solving skills, and preparing for a future where AI collaboration becomes an integral part of the development process. By adapting to these changes, developers will remain at the forefront of innovation, harnessing the full potential of AI to build more efficient, scalable, and intelligent software systems.

Conclusion

As we wrap up, it's clear that Cursor AI offers a transformative experience for developers, redefining how coding, debugging, and refactoring are approached in the modern development workflow. From real-time code suggestions to multi-file refactoring, and even turning design mockups into functional code, Cursor AI has proven itself to be a powerful tool that accelerates productivity and reduces the manual, repetitive tasks that often slow down the development process. By leveraging AI in these key areas, developers can focus more on creativity, high-level decision-making, and system design, knowing that Cursor AI is there to handle the details.

One of the most valuable lessons from using Cursor AI is the importance of collaboration between human intuition and AI-powered automation. Cursor doesn't replace the developer; instead, it acts as an intelligent assistant, constantly refining, suggesting, and improving code based on input. This allows developers to write cleaner, more efficient code in less time, enhancing both individual productivity and team collaboration. The ability to troubleshoot in real-time, with the AI offering context-aware suggestions, streamlines the debugging process, allowing issues to be resolved quickly and efficiently.

Cursor AI also showcases the potential for the future of coding, where design-to-code transitions, automated refactoring, and AI-driven optimizations are no longer the domain of manual effort but instead are handled by intelligent systems that understand the project holistically. This ability to seamlessly integrate changes across multiple files and functions makes codebases more maintainable and reduces the complexity involved in large-scale projects.

Moreover, the role of AI in managing back-end issues, especially with database connections and server-side interactions, further emphasizes its capability in handling complex, multi-layered problems. By automating these critical tasks, Cursor allows developers to focus on building features and improving user experiences rather than getting stuck in the weeds of server management or database optimization.

The future of AI in coding will likely expand on these features, and developers can prepare by continuing to explore how AI tools like Cursor can be integrated into their workflows. The more you use Cursor AI, the more you can unlock its potential, from enhancing UI layouts to optimizing database queries, all while ensuring that the code remains clean, scalable, and efficient. By embracing these AI-powered tools, developers can stay at the forefront of innovation in the tech industry, ready to adapt to even more advanced systems as they emerge.

With all this in mind, the next step is clear: it's time to implement Cursor AI into your projects. Whether you're working on a solo project or part of a larger development team, integrating AI tools like Cursor can dramatically improve the efficiency of your workflow. The benefits—faster development cycles, more accurate code, and streamlined collaboration—are tangible. As AI continues to evolve, the developers who embrace these tools now will be better prepared for the future of software development.

So, take the leap. Explore Cursor AI's full potential, test it out in your current project, and discover how it can simplify your development process, allowing you to focus on what truly matters: creating innovative, impactful software solutions. The future of coding is here, and AI is set to play a central role—don't miss the opportunity to be part of that evolution.

www.ingramcontent.com/pod-product-compliance
Lightning Source LLC
LaVergne TN
LVHW051702050326
832903LV00032B/3959